Berlitz®

101 *phrasal verbs* anglais en images

Berlitz Publishing
Paris • Munich • New York • Singapour

Berlitz 101 *phrasal verbs* anglais en images

Publié en France en 2007 par
Blay Foldex / Berlitz
40-48, rue des Meuniers
F-93108 MONTREUIL Cedex
Téléphone : 33 (0) 1 49 88 92 10
Fax : 33 (0) 1 49 88 92 09

Berlitz®

101
phrasal verbs
anglais
en images

Introduction

Le but de cet ouvrage est de rendre ludique et efficace l'apprentissage des *phrasal verbs* («verbes à particules») anglais sans le compliquer par nombre d'explications grammaticales superflues. En peu de temps, vous allez pouvoir mémoriser de nombreux *phrasal verbs* anglais, ainsi que leur traduction, grâce aux illustrations et aux exemples associés à chaque verbes, qui en fixent le sens. La particularité de cet ouvrage et des autres ouvrages de la collection **101 verbes en images** BERLITZ est d'être des manuels simples et agréables, tout en couleurs, pour un apprentissage des verbes qui ne soit enfin plus une torture !

Un ouvrage entièrement illustré

Les illustrations, du début à la fin de l'ouvrage, racontent une histoire : passez un moment à observer chaque image afin de bien vous en imprégner, vous constaterez que le *phrasal verb* anglais constituant le sens de chaque dessin sera ainsi beaucoup plus facilement mémorisable.

Les personnages sont récurrents, des intrigues se nouent et se dénouent au fil des 101 pages de verbes, chaque image livrant aussi des indices pour la compréhension des autres. Certaines seront plus complexes à déchiffrer que d'autres pour rendre ce décryptage plus amusant encore, mais aussi et surtout pour aider le processus de mémorisation.

La meilleure façon de se rappeler quelque chose est de procéder par association : la forme infinitive de chacun des 101 verbes anglais sélectionnés dans cet ouvrage a été dissimulée dans chacune des illustrations qui lui est associée. Ce procédé, et l'effort investi dans la recherche de cette forme infinitive dans l'image, agissent ainsi comme un signal de rappel, stimulant la mémoire à long terme : le verbe est désormais associé à une image amusante qui en fixe le sens dans la mémoire. Cette méthode d'apprentissage est de ce fait jusqu'à sept fois plus efficace que la lecture et la récitation passive d'une rébarbative liste de verbes ou d'un tableau de conjugaison.

Avoir des difficultés à mémoriser et à garder présent à l'esprit tout ce que l'on a appris d'une langue étrangère ne signifie pas que l'on a définitivement tout oublié, nous ne parvenons tout simplement pas à nous rappeler d'un nom, d'un verbe ou d'un temps au moment précis où on le voudrait. Cet ouvrage se propose d'aider efficacement chacun dans le processus d'apprentissage de la langue anglaise.

Plutôt que d'affronter avec répugnance et ennui des tableaux de verbes en noir et blanc, **101 *phrasal verbs* anglais en images** a été conçu pour faire de l'apprentissage des *phrasal verbs* un moment agréable par la stimulation et le divertissement des sens et non par leur engourdissement !

Vous pouvez également apprendre la conjugaison des verbes anglais, et ceux d'autres langues, grâce à l'ouvrage de cette même collection **101 verbes en images** Berlitz. Pour plus d'informations, pour pouvez consulter notre site internet **www.berlitzeditions.fr** ou nous écrire à l'adresse **info@berlitzeditions.fr**.

À propos de l'auteur

Rory Ryder a créé le concept des **101 *phrasal verbs* anglais en images** sur le constat que leur traitement dans les manuels destinés à leur apprentissage, était daté et inefficace. Pour la plupart des apprenants francophones, les «*phrasal verbs*» anglais, les fameux verbes à particules, sont une des difficultés majeures de la grammaire anglaise. La méthode classique consistant à les apprendre par cœur, ainsi que leur traduction, ne garantit nullement leur compréhension et leur réutilisation par la suite. Rory Ryder a ainsi développé cet ouvrage, qui rend la mémorisation et la compréhension des principaux *phrasal verbs* anglais simple, agréable et efficace. Il est également le concepteur et le créateur des ouvrages de la série des **101 verbes en images** Berlitz qui permettent un apprentissage ludique et efficace de la conjugaison des langues étrangères grâce notamment à l'accès Internet gratuit aux enregistrements de chaque forme verbale.

to look out faire attention, prendre garde

ONE DAY, A NATIVE AMERICAN INDIAN WARNS PEDRO AND MARIA TO LOOK OUT FOR DANGER.

- A ***look-out*** [*poste de guet*] can be a place to go and ***look out*** [*guetter*] for intruders.
- A person who is ***looking out*** [*surveiller*] for danger or intruders can also be called a ***look-out*** [*guetteur, vigie*].
- Someone can ***look out*** [*regarder dehors*] of a window.
- A person can say "***Look out***!" [*attention !*] if they want to warn somebody of danger.

to take aside

prendre à part

THE NATIVE AMERICAN INDIAN DECIDES TO TAKE PEDRO ASIDE AND WARN HIM THAT SOMETHING TERRIBLE IS GOING TO HAPPEN TO THE TIME MACHINE.

to tip off — prévenir, avertir

AS THE NATIVE AMERICAN INDIAN TIPS OFF PEDRO ABOUT HIS PREMONITION, PEDRO STARTS TO FEEL CONCERNED.

to tie up

ficeler, ligoter

PEDRO IS WORRIED, SO HE TIES UP THE TIME MACHINE.

to be left over

rester

LATER THAT DAY, THINGS SEEM TO BE GETTING WORSE FOR PEDRO. THE LANDLORD CALLS TO COLLECT MORE RENT. PEDRO HAS NO CHOICE; HE MUST GIVE ALL HIS LEFT OVER MONEY TO THE LANDLORD.

- When food is remaining after a meal, this is referred to as ***left-overs*** [*les restes*].

to close down fermer *(définitivement)*

PEDRO PAYS HIS RENT, BUT IS FORCED TO CLOSE DOWN HIS STUDIO AND LOOK FOR ANOTHER JOB.

to take on prendre, embaucher

AS PEDRO WALKS ON ALONG THE STREET, HE SEES A FAST FOOD RESTAURANT THAT IS TAKING ON NEW STAFF.

- A person can ***take*** [*accepter*] ***on*** responsibility.
- A boxer can ***take*** [*affronter*] ***on*** another contender.

to slip off

filer, s'éclipser

THE NEXT DAY MARIA IS CONFUSED WHEN EARLY THAT MORNING, PEDRO SLIPS OFF QUIETLY FOR WORK.

- It is very easy to ***slip off*** [*glisser*] a step when its iced over.
- A person ***slips off*** [*enlever rapidement*] their clothing if they're in a hurry.

to clock in

pointer *(à l'arrivée)*

WHEN PEDRO ARRIVES FOR HIS FIRST DAY AT WORK, HE NEEDS TO CLOCK IN THE TIME HE STARTS.

to sleep through

dormir
(sans être réveillé)

THAT EVENING PEDRO COMES HOME FROM WORK EXHAUSTED; HE GOES STRAIGHT TO BED, AND SLEEPS THROUGH ALL THE NOISE.

to slave away trimer

PEDRO WORKS VERY HARD, SLAVING AWAY AT THE FAST FOOD RESTAURANT, SERVING THE HUNGRY CUSTOMERS.

to pile up   s'accumuler, s'entasser

AS THE ORDERS FOR THE HAMBURGERS PILE UP, PEDRO WORKS HARDER AND HARDER.

- People can feel overwhelmed if they leave their unpaid bills ***to pile up*** [*s'accumuler*].
- A road accident involving more than two cars is a ***pile-up*** [*carambolage*].

to hurry up

se dépêcher

PEDRO WORKS FASTER THAN HE HAS EVER WORKED BEFORE, BUT HE IS STILL TOLD TO HURRY UP AND WORK EVEN FASTER.

to save up

économiser

LATER THAT DAY, PEDRO RETURNS HOME AND MARIA ASKS HIM WHAT IS WRONG. HE CONFESSES THAT HE HAS BEEN WORKING IN A FAST FOOD RESTAURANT TO PAY THE BILLS. MARIA TELLS PEDRO NOT TO WORRY BECAUSE SHE HAS BEEN SAVING UP.

to leave aside

laisser de côté

MARIA EXPLAINS TO PEDRO THAT IF SHE TAKES THE TIME MACHINE, SHE CAN GO BACK IN TIME TO SEE THE KING AND BRING BACK MORE MONEY FOR PEDRO TO OPEN HIS STUDIO AGAIN. PEDRO REMEMBERS WHAT THE NATIVE AMERICAN INDIAN SAID, AND TRIES TO LEAVE ASIDE THE CONVERSATION ABOUT THE TIME MACHINE AND TALK ABOUT SOMETHING DIFFERENT.

to talk through   expliquer, prévenir

NOT LISTENING, MARIA TAKES THE KEY FROM PEDRO. NOW PEDRO IS LEFT WITH NO CHOICE BUT TO TALK IT THROUGH WITH HER.
(PEDRO EXPLAINS THE WARNING)

to check over

examiner, vérifier

MARIA, UNCONVINCED, TELLS PEDRO TO CHECK OVER THE TIME MACHINE ONE MORE TIME. AFTER PEDRO HAS FINISHED CHECKING IT OVER HE GIVES MARIA THE THUMBS UP.

to fall apart

s'effondrer

SUDDENLY, THE TIME MACHINE BREAKS INTO PIECES AND FALLS APART.

- People can feel like they are ***falling apart*** [*craquer, perdre ses moyens*] when they are overworked or stressed.
- A business or organisation can ***fall apart*** [*sombrer*] if the workers walk out.

to do away with

se débarrasser, supprimer

PEDRO AND MARIA DECIDE TO DO AWAY WITH THE OLD TIME MACHINE, AND BUILD A NEW ONE.

- To ***do away with*** [*liquider, supprimer*] someone means to kill them.

to figure out

calculer, résoudre, comprendre

THAT AFTERNOON, PEDRO FIGURES OUT A NEW IDEA FOR YET ANOTHER TIME MACHINE!

- When somebody thinks they have all the answers, they can say "I have it all ***figured out*** [*résoudre*]".
- A person can ***figure out*** [*trouver, découvrir*] the direction by looking at a map.

to pull together

faire un effort

THE WHOLE FAMILY DECIDES TO PULL TOGETHER AND BUILD ANOTHER TIME MACHINE.

- People can be told to ***pull*** themselves ***together*** [*se ressaisir*] if they are finding it difficult to control their feelings.
- People can ***pull together*** [*joindre, réunir*] their ideas and suggestions to solve a problem.

to finish off

terminer, finir

AFTER A FEW DAYS, PEDRO AND MARIA FINISH OFF BUILDING THEIR EIGHTH TIME MACHINE AND CELEBRATE WITH A KISS.

to try out

essayer

PEDRO JUMPS INTO THE TIME MACHINE, AS HE CAN'T WAIT TO TRY IT OUT FOR THE FIRST TIME.

to come over

venir

LATER IN THE DAY, MARIA REMEMBERS THAT SHE WAS INVITED BY THE KING TO COME OVER FOR A CHAT.

- A feeling can ***come over*** [*saisir, s'emparer*] somebody in a particular situation.
- A message can *come over* [*provenir*] a loud speaker.
- She ***came over*** [*se sentir mal*] giddy.

to be related to

être parent

WHEN MARIA ARRIVES AT THE PALACE THE KING EXPLAINS THAT SHE IS RELATED TO HIM.

to stretch away   s'étendre

THE KING PROUDLY SHOWS MARIA HOW HIS LAND STRETCHES AWAY FOR AS FAR AS THE EYE CAN SEE.

to hand over

remettre, céder

THE KING DECLARES THAT HE IS TOO OLD TO BE KING, AND THAT HE WANTS TO HAND OVER THE CROWN TO MARIA.

- Responsibility can be ***handed over*** [*remettre*] from one person to another.
- A country can ***hand over*** [*céder*] its power.

to pour into remplir, verser à flots

MARIA EXPLAINS TO THE KING THAT SHE MUST GO BACK TO HER FAMILY. THE KING ORDERS HIS GUARDS TO POUR GOLD COINS INTO LARGE BAGS FOR MARIA TO TAKE BACK HOME.

- People ***pour into*** [*se ruer, affluer*] the shops when it's the first day of the sales.

to take away

emporter, enlever

MEANWHILE, BACK AT THE HOUSE PEDRO IS HAVING MORE PROBLEMS WHEN ALL THE FAMILY POSSESSIONS ARE TAKEN AWAY.

- Another name for a fast food restaurant is a ***take-away***.
- A judge might ask for the convicted thief to be ***taken away*** [*emmener, arrêter*].

to settle up

régler *(la note)*

WHEN MARIA RETURNS AND SEES THE GREEDY LANDLORD, SHE FLIPS A GOLD COIN INTO HIS HAND TO SETTLE UP ALL THE OUTSTANDING BILLS.

to keep on doing continuer à faire quelque chose

PEDRO IS NOW ABLE TO KEEP ON DOING HIS PAINTING, SCULPTING AND BUILDING, AND NO LONGER NEEDS HIS JOB IN THE FAST FOOD RESTAURANT.

to take in

prendre *(l'eau)*

ONE OF THE FIRST THINGS PEDRO BUILDS WHEN HE'S BACK IN HIS STUDIO IS A NEW BOAT. UNFORTUNATELY, IT TAKES IN WATER AND SLOWLY SINKS TO THE BOTTOM OF THE SEA.

- In the morning a person can open the front door and ***take in*** [*prendre*] the milk.
- Some hospitals ***take in*** [*recueillir, recevoir*] sick people.
- If a person wants their car fixed, they must ***take*** it ***in*** [*apporter*] to a garage.

to wrap up emballer, envelopper

LATER THAT DAY PEDRO WRAPS UP A PRESENT; IT'S A TIME MACHINE JEEP FOR MARIA.

- A person can ***wrap up*** [*s'habiller*] with more clothes to keep warm.
- People can be ***wrapped up*** [*absorber, empêtrer*] in their problems.
- Somebody can ***wrap up*** [*conclure*] a conversation by ending it quickly.

to pull ahead

prendre la tête

DELIGHTED WITH HER NEW TIME JEEP, MARIA PULLS AHEAD OF PEDRO IN A FRIENDLY RACE.

to be booked up

être occupé(e)

WHEN PEDRO RETURNS HOME LATER THAT DAY, HE ASKS MARIA IF SHE WOULD LIKE TO GO ON THE TIME BIKE FOR A QUICK TRIP BACK IN TIME. MARIA EXPLAINS SHE IS JUST TOO BOOKED UP.

- A hotel is ***booked up*** [*être complet*] when all the rooms are occupied.

to work out faire de la musculation

MARIA EXPLAINS TO PEDRO THAT SHE IS GOING TO WORK OUT AT THE GYM.

- A person can ***work out*** [*résoudre*] a mathematical problem.
- To find the answers you have to ***work out*** [*élucider*] the questions.
- If a negative situation is resolved you could say "everything ***worked out*** [*s'arranger*] in the end".

to leave behind

oublier, laisser

PEDRO LEAVES, AND MARIA CALLS HIM ON THE TIME BIKE PHONE TO TELL HIM NOT TO LEAVE BABY LUCA BEHIND.

- A person can ***leave behind*** [*oublier*] their problems.
- Somebody can ***leave behind*** [*laisser, ne pas emporter*] their keys.

to take through

expliquer

WHEN PEDRO RETURNS, MARIA TAKES HIM THROUGH ALL THE THINGS HE NEEDS TO DO WHEN HE IS LOOKING AFTER BABY LUCA.

to look up to

admirer

BABY LUCA LOOKS UP TO HIS DADDY WITH LOVE.

- A person can ***look up*** [*chercher, consulter*] a word in the dictionary.

to pick up prendre, ramasser

PEDRO PICKS UP LUCA, AND PUTS HIM ON HIS SHOULDERS.

- A taxi ***picks up*** [*passer, prendre*] passengers.
- The police like to ***pick up*** [*repérer, détecter*] bank robbers.
- A person can ***pick up*** [*attraper*] an illness.

to see off

dire au revoir

AS THE TIME MACHINE LEAVES MARIA SEES EVERYONE OFF BY WAVING HER HANDKERCHIEF.

to break down

tomber en panne

SUDDENLY, THE TIME MACHINE STARTS TO MAKE STRANGE NOISES AND BREAKS DOWN.

- People have a ***breakdown*** [*dépression*] when they become mentally ill.
- An arrangement or plan can ***break down*** [*rompre*] because of a disagreement.
- A ***breakdown*** [*rupture, interruption*] in communication between people can lead to all types of problems.
- Someone may ask for the figures to be ***broken down*** [*analyser, détailler*] before making their decision.

to get off prendre *(la route)*, partir

PEDRO DECIDES TO GET OFF THE ROAD QUICKLY TO AVOID TRAFFIC.

to fall down   tomber, s'effondrer

THIS TIME, WHEN PEDRO TRIES TO PUT BABY LUCA ON HIS SHOULDERS LUCA FALLS DOWN AND BANGS HIS HEAD.

- A building can ***fall down*** [*s'effondrer, s'écrouler*] after many years.
- In autumn/fall the leaves ***fall down*** [*tomber*] from the trees.

to burst into éclater, fondre *(en larmes)*

AS BABY LUCA BANGS HIS HEAD, HE BURSTS INTO TEARS.

- A person can ***burst into*** [*éclater de rire*] laughter when they find something very funny.
- Fireworks can ***burst into*** [*exploser*] hundreds of colours.
- The racecar ***burst into*** [*prendre feu, s'enflammer*] flames.

to bounce back renvoyer *(la balle)*

BABY LUCA DOES NOT WANT TO PLAY; HE HAS NO INTEREST IN BOUNCING THE BALL BACK.

- Undelivered emails can ***bounce back*** [*revenir, être refusé*].
- A person can ***bounce back*** [*se remettre*] from an illness or accident.

to cheer up

égayer, encourager

PEDRO TRIES TO CHEER UP BABY LUCA AND MAKE HIM LAUGH BY DOING SILLY THINGS WITH THE BALL.

to keep away ne pas s'approcher

AS PEDRO GOES TO REPAIR THE TIME MACHINE, BABY LUCA WANDERS OFF TO FIND HIS BALL. AS HE WALKS TOWARDS THE ANGRY MONKEY, HE DOESN'T SEE THE SIGN WARNING PEOPLE TO KEEP AWAY.

to scare away

faire fuir, effrayer

WHEN TOBIAS SEES WHERE BABY LUCA IS, HE RUNS TOWARDS THE ANGRY MONKEY TO SCARE HIM AWAY.

to look out for chercher, s'occuper de

AFTER PEDRO HAS FINISHED FIXING THE TIME MACHINE HES GOES TO LOOK OUT FOR BABY LUCA.

- When crossing a road, a mother can tell her child to ***look out for*** [*faire attention à*] traffic.

to track down *(finir par)* retrouver

FINALLY, AFTER SEARCHING IN MANY DIFFERENT PLACES, PEDRO TRACKS DOWN BABY LUCA.

to jump in

sauter dedans, plonger

LATER THAT AFTERNOON, PEDRO AND BABY LUCA GO SWIMMING. PEDRO TELLS BABY LUCA TO JUMP IN.

- A person can also ***jump in*** [*intervenir*] to a situation or conversation.

to go under

couler

LUCA JUMPS AND GOES UNDER THE WATER, BUT PEDRO IS THERE TO CATCH HIM.

- If a business ***goes under*** [*s'effondrer, faire faillite*], it becomes bankrupt.

to rely on

compter sur

LUCA SMILES AS HE KNOWS HE CAN RELY ON HIS DADDY TO BE THERE FOR HIM.

to fill up
faire le plein

AT THE END OF THE DAY PEDRO STOPS TO FILL UP THE TIME MACHINE WITH FUEL.

- When you ***fill*** something ***up*** [*remplir*] it becomes full.
- A football stadium can ***fill up*** [*se remplir*] with people.

to pull over

se ranger,
se garer sur le côté

AS THEY LEAVE THE FILLING STATION THEY ARE TOLD TO PULL OVER BY THE POLICE.

to lift off

décoller

PEDRO PRESSES THE BUTTON TO LIFT OFF AS THE POLICEMAN LOOKS ANGRILY AT HIM.

to wait up

patienter, veiller

MEANWHILE BACK AT THE HOUSE, MARIA IS WAITING UP FOR PEDRO AND BABY LUCA.

to show up

se montrer

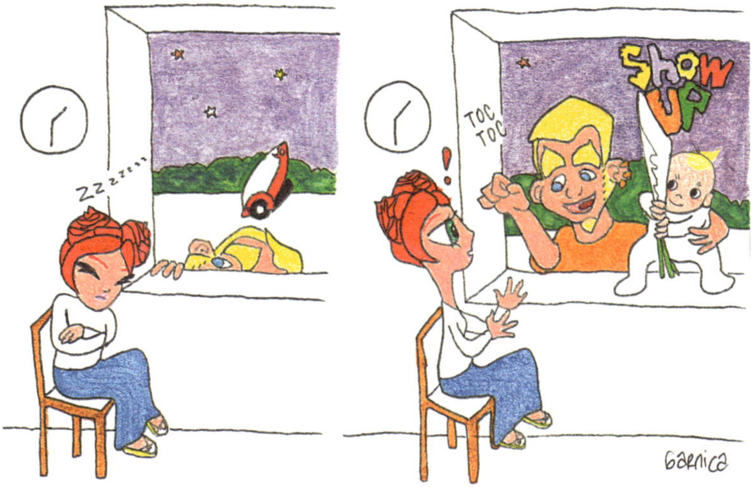

MARIA WAKES UP WHEN PEDRO AND LUCA FINALLY SHOW UP.

- A test or experiment can ***show up*** [*révéler, montrer*] results.
- You can ***show*** somebody ***up*** [*faire honte*] if you embarass them.

to take over

remplacer,
prendre la relève

MARIA IS HAPPY TO TAKE OVER FROM PEDRO.

to cloud over se couvrir, s'assombrir

THE NEXT MORNING PEDRO LOOKS UP AND SEES THE SKY CLOUDING OVER.

to pour down   pleuvoir à verse

WITHIN A FEW MINUTES THE RAIN BEGINS TO POUR DOWN.

to brighten up s'éclaircir, se dégager

AFTER HOURS OF RAIN, EVERYTHING STARTS TO BRIGHTEN UP WHEN THE SUN COMES OUT.

- Anyone can ***brighten up*** [*égayer*] a room with flowers.
- When people ***brighten up*** [*s'égayer, s'animer*], they look happier.

to set off partir, se mettre en route

ALL EXCITED, PEDRO SETS OFF ON A NEW JOURNEY ON HIS TIMEBIKE.

- When a bomb goes off it ***sets off*** [*déclencher*] a large explosion.
- A person can ***set*** someone ***off*** [*déclencher*] laughing or crying or complaining, etc.

to bring along

prendre,
amener avec soi

PEDRO PICKS UP VAN GOGH AND BRINGS HIM ALONG ON HIS TRAVELS.

to cross out rayer, barrer

PEDRO TAKES VAN GOGH FORWARD IN TIME TO MEET ANOTHER FAVORITE ARTIST WHO LIKES TO CROSS OUT HIS OWN WORK.

to hang out

fréquenter, traîner

PEDRO IS SO DELIGHTED THAT HE IS HANGING OUT WITH TWO OF HIS FAVORITE ARTIST.

• Somebody can ***hang out*** [*étendre, suspendre*] the washing.

to be caught up in être entraîné dans

PEDRO GOES BACK IN TIME WITH VAN GOGH AND THEY ARE CAUGHT UP IN A SITUATION THEY DON'T WANT TO BE IN.

to speak out parler en faveur, défendre

PEDRO TRIES TO SPEAK OUT, BUT THE PEOPLE DON'T WANT TO LISTEN.

to be snowed in

être bloqué

WHEN PEDRO AND VAN GOGH TRY TO LEAVE, THEY REALIZE THEY ARE SNOWED IN.

to turn to　　　se tourner vers

PEDRO TURNS TO THE SHERIFF FOR HELP, BUT THE SHERIFF LOOKS AWAY.

to walk out

sortir, partir

MEANWHILE BACK IN THE PRESENT DAY, MARIA WALKS OUT OF HER DANCE PERFORMANCE.

- When a factory or workplace go on strike, the workers ***walk out*** [*se mettre en grève*].

to call out for

appeler, faire appel

WHILE PEDRO IS CHASED BY THE ANGRY MOB, HE CALLS OUT FOR HELP FROM MARIA.

to hang up raccrocher

MARIA HANGS UP THE PHONE AND TURNS ON THE ENGINE.

- People can ***hang up*** [*suspendre, accrocher*] their hat and coat.

to well up avoir les larmes aux yeux

FEARING FOR PEDRO, MARIA'S EYES START TO WELL UP WITH TEARS.

to clear off

filer, décamper

AS MARIA PUTS HER TIME JEEP INTO REVERSE, SHE TELLS THE REPORTERS TO CLEAR OFF.

- If someone tells you to "***clear off***" [*dégager*], it's a rude way to say go away.

to stand up for défendre

MARIA ARRIVES AND STANDS UP FOR PEDRO AND VAN GOGH WHILE TOBIAS UNTIES THE ROPE.

to fight back se défendre, répondre

THE SHERIFF GRABS MARIA'S ARM AND CALLS HER A WITCH. MARIA KNOWS HER ONLY CHANCE IS TO FIGHT BACK.

- A person can ***fight back*** [*refouler*] an emotion or fear.

to help out

venir en aide,
tirer d'embarras

SUDDENLY THE NATIVE AMERICAN INDIAN APPEARS OUT OF NOWHERE TO HELP OUT.

to step on it appuyer sur l'accélérateur, se grouiller

WHEN THE SITUATION IS UNDER CONTROL, VAN GOGH TELLS PEDRO TO STEP ON IT*.

*** To *step on it* means to put your foot down on the excelerater.**

to get away

partir, s'en aller

WHEN EVERYBODY IS SAFELY IN THE TIME JEEP, PEDRO MAKES A QUICK GET AWAY.

- People can ***get away*** [*s'en aller, partir*] on holiday.

to come up with proposer, suggérer

A FEW MONTHS PASS BY AND PEDRO **COMES UP WITH** ANOTHER IDEA FOR A BACKPACK TIME MACHINE.

- If you ***come up with*** [*arriver à, arriver jusqu'à*] the right amount of money you can buy anything that's for sale.

to turn on

allumer

MARIA AND LUCA FIND IT FUNNY WHEN PEDRO TURNS ON HIS NEW BACKPACK TIME MACHINE.

to point out

montrer, indiquer

AS PEDRO TAKES HIS NEW TIME MACHINE BACK TO THE PAST, SOMEBODY POINTS OUT A STRANGE FLYING OBJECT.

- Someone can ***point out*** [*faire remarquer*] an important piece of information to another person.

to bring up

soulever,
mentionner *(un sujet)*

WHEN PEDRO TRIES TO BRING UP THE SUBJECT OF THE MONA LISA, LEONARDO DA VINCI BRINGS UP MATHEMATICS INSTEAD.

- A mother ***brings up*** [*élever*] her children.
- If you feel sick you may ***bring up*** [*vomir, rendre*] your food.

to get onto

aborder *(un sujet)*

PEDRO TRIES MANY TIMES TO GET ONTO THE SUBJECT OF THE MONA LISA.

- If a person needs to ***get on to*** [*se mettre en rapport, se mettre en contact*] someone they will be trying to contact them.

to come back to

revenir à

NOT PAYING ANY ATTENTION, LEONARDO COMES BACK TO MATHEMATICS.

to go on

continuer

PEDRO STARTS TO FEEL BORED AS LEONARDO GOES ON AND ON AND ON ABOUT MATHEMATICS.

to hold on

tenir bon

LEONARDO TRIES TO PROVE HIS MATHEMATICAL THEORIES, BUT PEDRO SHOUTS OUT "HOLD ON!"

- People can ***hold on*** [*s'accrocher à*] to an idea or belief about something.
- When people ***hold on*** [*garder*] to something they keep it longer than expected.
- If a person does not want to share something they may ***hold on*** [*retenir*] to it.

to read up on parcourir, lire en entier

PEDRO QUICKLY FLIES FORWARD IN TIME AND READS UP ON ALL THE FLYING INVENTIONS OF THE PAST.

to get back to revenir vers, rappeler

WHEN HE GETS BACK TO LEONARDO, HE GIVES THE ARTIST HIS FAVORITE BOOK ON INVENTIONS.

- When you return a phone call, you ***get back to*** [*rappeler, répondre*] someone.

to pass on transmettre

LEONARDO IS HAPPY WITH THIS GENEROUS GIFT AND DECIDES TO PASS ON THE SECRETS OF THE MONA LISA TO PEDRO.

- When you have finished using something you can ***pass** it **on*** [*passer*].
- Traditions are ***passed on*** [*transmettre*] from generation to generation.
- If somebody ***passes on*** [*décéder*] they have died.

to read out

lire à haute voix

AFTER PEDRO RETURNS HOME,
HE DECIDES TO READ OUT THE WORDS
OF WISDOM TO ALL THE PEOPLE.

to put up

affricher, accrocher

WHEN PEDRO HAS FINISHED READING OUT THE WORDS OF WISDOM, HE PUTS THEM UP ON THE WALL FOR EVERYONE TO SEE.

- Some people are forced to ***put up*** [*supporter*] with terrible conditions.
- A building can be ***put up*** [*construire, ériger*].
- A person can ***put up*** [*s'opposer, résister*] a fight if they believe in something.

to pass for   se faire passer pour

AS PEDRO PREPARES FOR ANOTHER TIME MACHINE JOURNEY BACK IN TIME, HE IS UNAWARE OF THE GAMBLER AND THE THIEF, WHO ARE PASSING FOR SUITCASES.

- The actor ***passes for*** [*passer pour*] a real king when he is in costume.

to weigh down

alourdir

WHEN THE TIME MACHINE TAKES OFF, PEDRO NOTICES THAT SOMETHING IS WEIGHING IT DOWN.

- Somebody can be ***weighed down*** [*être surchargé*] with work or committments.

to mouth off

se vanter,
parler à tort et à travers

WHEN PEDRO DISCOVERS THE PROBLEM, EVERYBODY IN THE TIME BUBBLE IS FORCED TO HEAR THE GAMBLER MOUTHING OFF.

to drop off

déposer, laisser

AS THE TIME BUBBLE FLIES OVER LAS VEGAS, PEDRO THINKS IT'S THE PERFECT PLACE TO DROP OFF THE GAMBLER AND THE THIEF.

to go off sonner, se déclencher

WITHIN NO TIME THE ALARMS IN LAS VEGAS ARE GOING OFF.

- A gun or bomb can ***go off*** [*se déclencher, tirer*].
- Somebody can ***go off*** [*se détacher, ne plus aimer*] another person.
- A person can ***go off*** [*aller dormir*] to sleep.

to bring before amener, comparaître

SOON THE THIEF IS BROUGHT BEFORE THE JUDGE AND THE SENTENCE IS PASSED.

to end up — se terminer, finir

FINALLY, PEDRO, MARIA, BABY LUCA AND TOBIAS ALL END UP ON ANOTHER ADVENTURE JOURNEY BACK IN TIME.

TO BE CONTINUED...

INDEX